Board of Governors of the Federal Reserve System
Office of the Comptroller of the Currency
Federal Deposit Insurance Corporation

# Guide to the Interagency Country Exposure Review Committee Process

## November 2008

# Table of Contents

| | Page |
|---|---|
| Background | 1 |
| Transfer Risk, Country Risk, and Credit Risk | 3 |
| Purpose of the Committee | 3 |
| Composition of the Committee | 4 |
| Frequency of Meetings | 4 |
| Countries Reviewed by the ICERC | 4 |
| The ICERC Rating System | 5 |
| The ICERC Process | 6 |
| Evaluating Transfer Risk | 6 |
| Application of ICERC Ratings | 7 |
| Special Categories of Exposure | 8 |
| Allocated Transfer Risk Reserve Requirement | 9 |
|     Reducing the ATRR Requirement | 10 |
|     ATRR Rulings and Interpretations | 10 |
| Country Write-ups | 12 |
|     Production and Updating | 12 |
|     Content | 13 |
|     Distribution | 13 |
|     Discontinuing Country Write-ups | 14 |

## Appendices

A. Excerpt from the Instructions for Preparation of the FFIEC 009 Country Exposure Report ........ 15
B. Abridged Preamble to the *Federal Register* Publication of the ATRR Regulation ........ 21
C. Interagency Statement on the Treatment of Debt-for-Equity and Debt-for-Debt Exchanges ........ 28

# Background

The international banking activities of U.S. banks are supervised by several of the federal banking agencies: the Office of the Comptroller of the Currency (OCC), the Federal Deposit Insurance Corporation (FDIC), and the Federal Reserve System; and by the appropriate state banking agencies. Among other things, the agencies evaluate the quality and liquidity of each bank's foreign exposures to determine their effect on the solvency and overall condition of the bank.

In 1979, the OCC, the FDIC, and the Federal Reserve Board established the Interagency Country Exposure Review Committee (ICERC, or the committee) to ensure consistent treatment of the transfer risk associated with banks' foreign exposures to both public- and private-sector entities. Transfer risk is the possibility that an asset cannot be serviced in the currency of payment because of a lack of, or restraints on the availability of, needed foreign exchange in the country of the obligor.

In the early 1980s, a growing number of problem foreign loans led the U.S. Congress to pass the International Lending Supervision Act of 1983 (ILSA), which included provisions affecting both the international lending activities of U.S. banks and the federal banking agencies' supervision of those activities. ILSA required banks, in certain circumstances, to set up an allocated reserve for assets subject to severe transfer risk, and in early 1984 the three federal banking agencies published regulations implementing the allocated transfer risk reserve (ATRR) requirement. The regulations require that each affected bank charge off or establish and maintain an ATRR for each asset with impaired value due to transfer risk. (See 12 CFR 28, Subpart C; 12 CFR 211, Subpart D; or 12 CFR 347.)

Notwithstanding the 2007-08 credit crisis, the federal banking agencies recognize the improvements that have been made in banks' cross-border exposure analysis. Specifically, since the implementation of ILSA, banks

- Improved their sovereign risk management practices;
- Developed better approaches for analysis and assessment of sovereign risk; and
- Enhanced their ability to monitor, manage, and control sovereign credit risk, including the establishment of limits by country and sovereign obligor.

Furthermore, international accounting and reporting standards have improved in the intervening years, resulting in greater transparency in financial disclosure by governments and public-sector obligors.

As a consequence, the federal agencies have reassessed the ICERC procedures and adjusted the criteria for assigning ICERC ratings. The agencies have reformed and modernized the ICERC process by effecting the following changes:

**1. Rate only those countries in default.**

Previously, ICERC reviewed and rated all countries to which U.S. banks had either an aggregate exposure of $1 billion or more for at least two consecutive quarters, or an aggregate exposure of between $200 million and $1 billion if the exposure at five or more U.S. banks exceeded 25 percent of their capital. Rating only defaulted countries will significantly reduce the burden on banks, while continuing to meet ILSA standards.

Default occurs when a country is not complying with its external debt-service obligations or is unable to service the existing loan according to its terms, as evidenced by failure to pay principal and interest fully and on time, arrearages, forced restructuring, or rollovers. The Committee reserves the right to exclude de minimis failures to pay principal and interest, such as incidences of technical or administrative defaults.

**2. Eliminate the rating categories of Other Transfer Risk Problems (OTRP), Weak, Moderately Strong, and Strong.**

The OTRP risk category was used for countries that were not meeting their external debt-service obligations, but were taking positive steps to restore debt service through economic adjustment measures, generally as part of an International Monetary Fund (IMF) program. The category also was used in some instances as a signal of possible deterioration, as when a country was meeting its debt obligations but noncompliance appeared imminent.

The ICERC has eliminated the OTRP rating. In addition, the ICERC has eliminated all Pass subcategories (i.e., Weak, Moderately Strong, and Strong) because countries with these ratings were not at imminent risk of default or other transfer risk event.

**3. Request that the Federal Reserve Bank of New York provide written analyses only on defaulted countries and, in addition, prepare regional and country overviews for selected areas in emerging markets as requested by the Committee.**

Previously, the Federal Reserve Bank of New York prepared analyses on all countries in the Moderately Strong, Weak, and OTRP categories. Since such categories have been eliminated, the regional overview will focus analytical skill and attention on areas of increasing risk, thus making the ICERC process more efficient and relevant.

## Transfer Risk, Country Risk, and Credit Risk

Transfer risk is one facet of the more broadly defined concept of "country risk." Country risk, which has an overarching effect on the realization of an institution's foreign assets, encompasses all of the uncertainties arising from the economic, social, and political conditions in a country. Country risk includes the possibility of deteriorating economic conditions, political and social upheaval, nationalization and expropriation of assets, government repudiation of external indebtedness, exchange controls, and rapid currency depreciation or devaluation. While ICERC-assigned transfer risk ratings focus narrowly on the availability of foreign exchange to service a country's external debt, an institution's own internal country risk management process should focus on the more broadly defined concept of country risk.

Country risk is also an important consideration when evaluating the level of credit risk associated with individual counterparties in a country. Regardless of the availability of foreign exchange, macroeconomic conditions and events that are beyond the control of individual borrowers can strain or impair the financial capacity of otherwise sound credit risks. Significant depreciation of a country's exchange rate, for example, increases the cost of servicing external debt and can adversely affect not only transfer risk for the country, but also the credit risk associated with even the strongest counterparties in the country.

## Purpose of the Committee

The ICERC is responsible for providing an assessment of the degree of transfer risk that is inherent in the cross-border and cross-currency exposures of U.S. banks. Although banks are advised of the results of the ICERC's evaluations, the ICERC's transfer risk ratings are primarily a supervisory tool and should not replace a bank's own country risk analysis process.

Supervisors expect institutions under their supervision to continue to monitor closely their cross-border exposure to all countries; to have robust country risk assessment systems; to have appropriate sovereign exposure limits in place for each sovereign entity; to perform solid financial analysis on the sovereign entities to which the institutions are exposed; and, generally, to continue to apply sound risk management to all of their cross-border exposures, not just to the countries rated by ICERC. Such risk management functions will continue to be evaluated during the course of regular supervisory examinations.

## Composition of the Committee

The ICERC is composed of nine voting members (primarily, experienced international bank examiners), with three representatives from three of the federal banking agencies: the OCC, FDIC, and the Federal Reserve System. In addition, representatives from the Conference of State Bank Supervisors and the Office of Thrift Supervision attend the committee's meetings as observers. Responsibility for chairing the meetings rotates among the three agencies annually. A staff member from the OCC serves as the committee's permanent Secretariat.

## Frequency of Meetings

The ICERC meets annually, in October, to review and assign transfer risk ratings, as applicable, to exposures. The committee also endeavors to hold a conference call in April to discuss any emerging issues or procedural matters. The committee reserves the option to meet intermittently throughout the year as circumstances warrant.

## Countries Reviewed by the ICERC

The ICERC reviews defaulted countries to which U.S. banks have had an aggregate exposure of $1 billion or more for at least two consecutive quarters. In addition, countries to which aggregate exposure is between $200 million and $1 billion are reviewed by the ICERC if the exposure at five or more U.S. banks exceeds 25 percent of capital (Tier 1 capital + the allowance for loan and lease losses). For purposes of determining whether a country meets the threshold for review by the ICERC, aggregate exposure is based on the exposure reported in the most recent Country Exposure Lending Survey.[1] Specifically, aggregate exposure is the sum of "Transfer Risk Claims" from Table 1 and "Unused Commitments" and "Guarantees and Credit Derivatives" from Table 2.[2]

If a country in default does not meet at least one of the exposure criteria for two consecutive quarters, the committee decides whether it should continue to be reviewed

---

[1] The E.16 Country Exposure Lending Survey report, which is published quarterly by the Federal Financial Institutions Examination Council (FFIEC), summarizes the aggregate, by-country exposures of U.S. banks, bank holding companies, and Edge and Agreement corporations filing the FFIEC 009 regulatory reporting form ("Country Exposure Report"). The E.16 report is available to the public on the FFIEC website at http://www.ffiec.gov/e16.htm.

[2] The "Guarantees and Credit Derivatives" component captures the notional value of credit derivatives sold. This measure is a conservative estimate of contingent liabilities where a bank has taken exposure to a referenced credit in the given country. Netting does not take place in the reporting of credit derivatives since counterparty positions may not offset.

based on the number of banks with exposure, and the trend of conditions in the country.

## The ICERC Rating System

The ICERC's assessment of transfer risk reflects the committee's application of the following category definitions:

**Substandard.** This category applies when a country is not complying with its external debt-service obligations as evidenced by arrearages, forced restructuring, or rollovers; and if either of the two following conditions exist:

- The country is not in the process of adopting an IMF or other suitable economic adjustment program, or is not adequately adhering to such a program; or
- The country and its bank creditors have not negotiated a viable rescheduling and are unlikely to do so in the near future.

**Value Impaired.** This category applies when a country has protracted arrearages, as indicated by more than one of the following:

- The country has not fully paid its interest for six months.
- The country has not complied with IMF programs and there is no immediate prospect for compliance.
- The country has not met rescheduling terms for more than one year.
- The country shows no definite prospects for an orderly restoration of debt service in the near future.

**Loss.** This category applies when the loan is considered uncollectible and of such little value that its continuance as a bankable asset is not warranted. An example would be an outright repudiation by a country of its obligations to banks, the IMF, or other lenders.

As discussed in more detail in the "Allocated Transfer Risk Reserve Requirement" section below, exposures rated as "Value Impaired" are generally subject to an ATRR requirement. Aggregate exposures rated "Substandard" are relevant to any assessment of possible concentrations of risk, and certainly should be factored into the evaluation of the adequacy of the bank's capital and allowance for loan and lease losses.

## The ICERC Process

The ICERC bases its assessments and ratings on information collected from a number of sources, including detailed country studies prepared by economists at the Federal Reserve Bank of New York. The studies focus on economic, social, and political risk factors in a country and provide statistical information about a country's external debt, balance of payments, and general economic conditions.

Prior to each meeting, examiners and economists from the federal banking agencies visit U.S. banks with significant international exposures to discuss economic conditions and political developments in specific countries with the banks' country risk management executives and staff. The examiners also inquire about the banks' lending terms and their strategic plans concerning the types of exposures and the desired mix and level of exposure in a country.

Finally, the ICERC draws on other U.S. government sources to supplement and confirm the information it has gathered on a country. Among other things, these sources can provide information on any bilateral or multilateral financial assistance that a country may be seeking or receiving.

## Evaluating Transfer Risk

The committee's evaluation of transfer risk for assigning the appropriate ICERC rating and, if applicable, ATRR (as discussed below in the "Allocated Transfer Risk Reserve Requirement" section) is influenced by a country's anticipated current account performance and debt service in relation to such factors as available IMF facilities, international reserve levels, the existence (if any) of exchange controls, official and private loan commitments, foreign investment trends, and the attitude among bankers toward further lending to borrowers in that country.

The committee also evaluates the socio-political effects of prevailing economic trends and their impact on a country's prospective ability to sustain external debt service. The committee considers such factors as the country's total external debt size and structure in relation to revenues, projections of volume and price for commodity exports, ability to attract foreign investment, natural and human resource potential, and willingness and ability of the government to recognize economic or budgetary problems and implement appropriate remedial action.

## Application of ICERC Ratings

ICERC transfer risk ratings are applicable in:

- Every U.S.-chartered, insured commercial bank in the 50 states of the United States, the District of Columbia, Puerto Rico, and U.S. territories and possessions;
- Every U.S. bank holding company, including its Edge and agreement corporations and other domestic and foreign nonbank subsidiaries; and
- The U.S. branches and agencies of foreign banks (however, the ATRR requirement does not apply to these entities).

In general, ICERC ratings are applicable to all types of foreign assets held by an institution, with the exception of premises, other real estate owned, and goodwill. For purposes of the ICERC rating, the determination of where the transfer risk for a particular exposure lies takes into consideration the existence of any guarantees and is based on the country of residence of the ultimate obligor as determined in accordance with the instructions for the FFIEC 009 Country Exposure Report form. (Relevant excerpts from these instructions, effective March 2006, can be found in Appendix A.)

Except as noted in footnote 3, the ICERC transfer risk rating is the only rating applicable to sovereign exposures in a reviewed country (that is, direct or guaranteed obligations of the country's central government or government-owned entities).[3] Furthermore, except as noted in the following paragraph, the ICERC transfer risk rating is the minimum risk rating applicable to all other cross-border and cross-currency exposures of U.S. banks in a reviewed country.

However, regardless of the currencies involved, to the extent that an institution's claims on local country residents are funded by liabilities to local country residents, the ICERC's transfer risk ratings do not apply. For example, to the extent that it has liabilities to local residents (such as sterling deposits), claims of the London branch of a U.S. bank on a public or private sector obligor in the United Kingdom (whether they be denominated in sterling, dollars, or Euros) are not subject to the ICERC transfer risk rating.

The ICERC is not able to evaluate the credit risk associated with individual, private-sector exposures in a country. Therefore, based on an evaluation of credit risk factors (including the effects of country risk), examiners may assign credit risk ratings to

---

[3] However, if they are carried on the institution's books as an investment, securities issued by a sovereign entity are also subject to the FFIEC's "Uniform Agreement on the Classification of Assets and Appraisal of Securities Held by Banks and Thrifts." The FFIEC agreement provides for specific, and possibly more severe, classification treatment of "sub-investment quality securities."

individual, private-sector exposures that are more severe than the ICERC-assigned transfer risk rating for the country. For any given private-sector exposure, the applicable rating is the more severe of either the ICERC-assigned transfer risk rating for the country or the examiner-assigned credit risk rating (including ratings assigned as a result of the Shared National Credit Program).

Questions sometimes arise concerning the consideration that examiners should give to informal expressions of support by the central government of a country for a particular borrower or sector of the economy (most often, banking). Unless such an expression of support constitutes a guarantee or other legally binding commitment, examiners should view it as no more than a mitigating factor in their evaluation of the counterparty's credit risk. Informal expressions of support by the central government would not cause the counterparty's credit risk rating to revert to the ICERC-assigned transfer risk rating for the country.

## Special Categories of Exposure

Although the ICERC may have rated ordinary short- and/or long-term exposures in a country as "Substandard," "Value Impaired," or "Loss," there are several special categories of exposure in a country that may receive a less-severe transfer risk rating if certain conditions are met.

- **Performing short-term bank and performing short-term trade exposures.**[4]
  Short-term bank and trade exposures are generally considered to have a lower level of transfer risk because, historically, they have received priority in the allocation of a country's foreign-exchange resources. In recognition of their historical performance, the ICERC usually assigns a more favorable rating to these types of exposures.

---

[4] A **performing credit** is current and has not been restructured to avoid delinquency or because of a deterioration in the financial condition of the borrower. A credit is considered to be current if it would not be reported as "past due" or "nonaccrual" as those terms are defined in the instructions for schedule RC-N of the FFIEC 031/041 reporting forms (Call Report).

The definition of **banks** is the same as is used for column 1 of the FFIEC 009 Country Exposure Report form. It includes commercial banks, savings banks, discount houses, and other similar institutions accepting short-term deposits. It also includes banking institutions owned by foreign governments unless such institutions function as central banks or banks of issue.

A **short-term credit** has a maturity of one year or less. Short-term credits are reported in column 7 of the FFIEC 009 Country Exposure Report form.

**Trade credit** consists of credit extensions that are directly related to imports or exports and will be liquidated through the proceeds of international trade. Such credit extensions will include pre-export financing **only** where there is a firm export sales order and the proceeds of the order will pay off the indebtedness. Trade credits are reported in column 6 of Schedule 1A of the FFIEC 009 Country Exposure Report form.

- **Securities held in trading accounts.** Presuming that there is an active and liquid market for the securities and the bank has procedures in place to appropriately value them, the ICERC may, on a case-by-case basis, assign a less-severe transfer risk rating to specific securities held in the bank's trading account. In any case, because Financial Accounting Standard No. 115 requires that they be marked-to-market, trading account securities are not subject to an ATRR requirement.

- **Direct equity investments.** The ICERC may, on a case-by-case basis, assign a less-severe transfer risk rating to specific, direct equity investments where all of the following conditions are met:

    1. The investment has been marked-to-market or is valued using the equity accounting method;

    2. The institution has provided the ICERC with evidence that the foreign business is financially viable; and

    3. The institution has provided the ICERC with evidence of its ability to repatriate dividends, interest payments, and proceeds from the sale of assets on a timely basis.

## Allocated Transfer Risk Reserve Requirement[5]

For each country exposure rated "Value Impaired," the ICERC recommends an appropriate percentage level for the ATRR. The ATRR is a specific reserve that is created by a charge to current income. The ATRR, which is not counted in the bank's capital, is separate from the allowance for loan and lease losses (ALLL) and is deducted from gross loans and leases.

When approved by the principals of the three federal banking agencies, the amount of the ATRR requirement is communicated to each bank that has reported exposures to the subject country. A bank's compliance with the ATRR requirement is measured on an asset-by-asset basis rather than a portfolio-wide basis. Except as noted in the following paragraph and in the subsection below on "ATRR Rulings and Interpretations," each exposure rated "Value Impaired" in a country must be specifically provided for in the required percentage.

The ATRR is required to be established by banks, bank holding companies, and Edge and agreement corporations on a consolidated basis in accordance with the procedures and tests of significance set forth in the instructions for preparation of Call Reports or other federal regulatory record keeping, reporting, and disclosure requirements. As an

---

[5] This section summarizes the most important aspects of the ATRR requirement. For further information, see the abridged preamble to the *Federal Register* publication of the ATRR regulation in Appendix B. Among other things, the preamble discusses: (1) assets to be covered by the ATRR, (2) applicability to nonbank and foreign subsidiaries, (3) criteria for requiring an ATRR, (4) percentage norms, and (5) treatment of ATRR accounting.

alternative to establishing an ATRR, an institution may write down the value of the specified international assets in the requisite amount. Such assets may be written down by a charge to the ALLL or a reduction in the principal amount of the asset by applying interest payments or other collections on the asset. However, if this alternative accounting treatment is used, the institution may not write up the value of the assets if the ATRR requirement is later reduced or eliminated.

## Reducing the ATRR Requirement

An ICERC decision to reduce the ATRR requirement and to upgrade exposures in a country from "Value Impaired" status will be based on the country meeting all of the following criteria:

- Orderly debt service has been restored for at least one year;
- Transfer-risk-related arrears to commercial banks have been eliminated and there is no expectation that the arrears will recur; and
- The country has demonstrated sustainable, improved economic performance through successful implementation of an IMF program or other suitable economic adjustment program.

Generally, at the first ICERC meeting following the satisfaction of these conditions, the committee reduces substantially the level of the ATRR requirement. The next time the country is reviewed, the remaining ATRR requirement is eliminated, and the transfer risk rating for exposures to the country is upgraded.

## ATRR Rulings and Interpretations

Although the general rule is that all exposures rated "Value Impaired" are subject to the ATRR requirement, over the years a number of clarifications and refinements of this rule have been made. These clarifications, which began with the explanatory preamble to the original ATRR regulation (included as Appendix B), include the following:

**An ATRR is required only for international assets that are subject to transfer risk.** The preamble to the regulation clearly states that the following categories of exposures would normally not be subject to the ATRR requirement:

- Assets of which the performance of the direct obligor is guaranteed by a resident of another country, unless exposures to the guarantor are also rated as "Value Impaired." (In this situation, the applicable transfer risk rating is determined by the country of the guarantor, who is the ultimate obligor.)

- Certain collateralized assets, of which full payment will come from proceeds that can be accessed outside the country of the direct obligor. (This situation generally arises in connection with loans to the exporter of a commodity, such as oil, where arrangements have been made for the buyer to deposit payments in another country.)

An ATRR is not required for off-balance sheet, potential exposures, such as unfunded commitments.

In addition, the preamble to the regulation indicates that the agencies would "...consider whether the performance characteristics of certain other categories of assets are such that no ATRR is warranted against those assets (for example, assets on which debt service has been maintained with little or no interruption)." As noted in the section above on "Special Categories of Exposure," for countries in which most other exposures are rated "Value Impaired," the ICERC generally assigns a less-severe transfer risk rating to performing short-term trade and bank credits, thereby eliminating the ATRR requirement for those assets.

**The ATRR requirement does not apply to U.S. branches, agencies, or commercial lending company subsidiaries of foreign banking organizations.** Nevertheless, each federal banking agency will determine the need, if any, for other special measures that may be warranted by conditions in the branch, including, for example, increased monitoring of due-from/due-to head office accounts, asset maintenance requirements, and/or specific reserves.

**Assets of an investment Edge corporation do not require an ATRR.** In a 1997 letter, the committee confirmed that an ATRR is required only on the assets of a "banking institution" as defined in 12 CFR 28, 12 CFR 211, and 12 CFR 347 (including a domestic U.S. bank, Edge, or agreement corporation *engaged in banking*). An Edge corporation that does not accept deposits in the United States from nonaffiliated persons (i.e., an investment Edge corporation) is not considered to be engaged in banking and is, therefore, not subject to the ATRR requirement.

**As long as they are performing, advances that originate after the ICERC's initial assignment of a "Value Impaired" rating to exposures in a country (i.e., "net new lending") are not subject to the ATRR requirement.** Relief from the ATRR requirement for such advances is based on the presumption that a bank will not increase its exposure in the country unless it has taken special measures to mitigate transfer risk. However, any such advances that fail to perform as originally agreed automatically become subject to the ATRR requirement. (See the definition of a "performing credit" in footnote 4 to the earlier discussion of "Special Categories of Exposure.")

In addition to relief from the ATRR requirement, if and when the ICERC determines that a country has initiated a suitable economic adjustment program, the committee establishes a "cut-off" date after which net new lending is eligible for more favorable rating treatment by the committee. Ratings for net new lending originating after the cut-off date are decided by the ICERC on a case-by-case basis. Continuation of the more favorable rating treatment for net new lending is evaluated by the committee each time the country is reviewed. Net new lending that does not perform as originally agreed on is automatically downgraded to "Value Impaired" and becomes subject to the ATRR requirement.

**Applicability of ATRRs to debt-for-equity or debt-for-debt exchanges**. Because transfer risk may continue to exist for an exposure converted to (or exchanged for) assets in the form of equity or debt securities, the agencies issued an interagency policy statement in 1992 concerning the applicability of ATRRs to these types of exposure. The policy statement, which can be found in Appendix C, includes the following additional guidance concerning the ATRR requirement:

- The initial recorded value of a security received in a debt conversion cannot exceed the carrying value of the converted loan exposure, net of any applicable ATRR.

- Because they are required to be carried at market value, securities that are held in a bank's trading account (i.e., for which there is an active and liquid market) and that are traded actively by the bank in a U.S.-dollar or other hard-currency market are exempt from the ATRR.

- In all other cases, including both securities held for investment purposes and those that are "available for sale," the ATRR framework applies <u>unless</u> the ICERC determines in its review of transfer risk for a particular country that grounds exist for a more favorable treatment of securities obtained in officially sanctioned debt conversion programs in that country.

# Country Write-ups

## Production and Updating

Write-ups are generated or updated only when a country has been discussed and voted on by the ICERC. The date appearing just below the country name at the top of each write-up is the date of the last review and update of that country.

## Content

Each country write-up has four sections: a rating matrix, an introductory summary, a description of the situation at that time, and supporting comments for the assigned rating.

The *rating matrix* that appears at the top of each write-up summarizes ICERC ratings for the country by exposure type; typically these are performing short-term bank credits, performing short-term trade credits, and all other exposures. Rating categories used in the matrix are "Not Rated," "Substandard," "Value Impaired," and "Loss."

The *introductory summary* provides information on the aggregate amount and nature of U.S. bank exposures to the subject country. In addition to noting any trend in the overall level of aggregate exposure, this section provides information on the distribution of exposures, including the amount of direct outstandings, commitments,[6] trade-related exposures, trading assets, net local country exposures, and net revaluation gains. Information also is provided on the by-sector and by-maturity distribution of U.S. bank exposures. Any available information on the existence/level of arrears also is included in this section. When drafting this section, the ICERC ensures that any information concerning arrears or bank attitudes toward lending comes from publicly available sources.

The *description of the situation at the time* summarizes conditions in the country at that time, notes any improvement or deterioration in conditions since the previous write-up, and identifies any specific issues of concern. When appropriate, the section also includes specific comments on the country's access to capital markets, as well as the condition of the banking system.

The *supporting comments* section includes the date of the previous rating and identifies the specific reasons and conditions justifying the assigned ICERC rating. When there has been an upgrade or a downgrade in the rating, the specific areas of improvement or deterioration are noted. This section also provides information on any ATRR requirement and the reasons for any change in the requirement. Where applicable, the section includes the cut-off date and rating for new money advances.

## Distribution

Because the ICERC deliberations are a part of the examination process, the committee's transfer risk ratings can be communicated only to those institutions that have exposures to the reviewed country. Following each ICERC meeting, write-ups

---

[6] The category "commitments" includes guarantees and credit derivatives (notional amount sold).

are generated for rated countries and routinely provided to banks, bank holding companies, and Edge and agreement corporations that have reported exposure to the country on the most recent FFIEC 009 Country Exposure Report form.[7]

Because they are not required to file a FFIEC 009 Country Exposure Report form, some smaller U.S. banks and the U.S. branches and agencies of foreign banks do not receive country write-ups as a result of the routine distribution that follows each ICERC meeting. In addition, some institutions may have exposures that were not reported on the FFIEC 009 Country Exposure Report form, either because they were booked after the quarterly reporting date or were less than the reporting threshold (all amounts on the report are rounded to the nearest million U.S. dollars). In these cases, the institution may make a request to its supervising office for a copy of the country write-ups applicable to its exposures.

## Discontinuing Country Write-ups

When no further write-ups are to be issued for a country of which exposures had been rated previously, the remaining banks with exposure to the country are notified in writing that the previous ICERC rating is no longer in effect and the reason the exposures are no longer reviewed.

---

[7] Specific reporting requirements can be found in the instructions for the FFIEC 009 Country Exposure report form. In general, the report is required to be filed quarterly:
- By every U.S.-chartered commercial bank that has aggregate foreign claims of more than $30 million and a foreign branch, international banking facility, or majority-owned subsidiary.
- Under certain conditions, by bank holding companies.
- By Edge and Agreement corporations with claims on foreign residents exceeding $30 million, except if they are majority-owned by a commercial bank that files on a consolidated basis.

# Appendix A

# Excerpt from the Instructions for Preparation of the FFIEC 009 Country Exposure Report[8]

## PART II – REPORTING DEFINITIONS

### A. Claims

The term "claims" follows the definition in the instructions for preparation of the FFIEC 031 and FR Y-9C including the following types of assets:

- Deposit balances, both interest bearing and non-interest bearing, held at banks in foreign countries, foreign branches of other U.S. banks, foreign branches of foreign banks, and U.S. branches of foreign banks
- Balances with foreign central banks and foreign official institutions
- Foreign securities
- Federal funds sold to foreigners, U.S. branches of foreign banks, or other U.S. entities that are branches of a foreign company
- Loans to or guaranteed by non-U.S. addressees
- Holdings of acceptances of foreign banks
- Foreign direct lease financing
- Investments in unconsolidated foreign subsidiaries and associated companies
- Positive fair value of interest rate, foreign exchange, equity, commodity and other derivative contracts with non-U.S. addressees (Reported in schedule 2)
- Customers' liability on acceptances outstanding where the account party is foreign
- Accrued income receivables from or guaranteed by non-U.S. addressees (including interest, commissions and income earned or accrued and applicable to current or prior periods, but not yet collected)
- Resale agreements and other financing agreements with non-U.S. addressees
- Asset sales with recourse with non-U.S. addressees
- Participations and syndications of loans to non-U.S. addressees

Premises, Other Real Estate Owned, and Goodwill should be excluded from claims for the purposes of this report.

---

[8] These instructions, which were current as of the publication of this document, went into effect in March 2006. The FFIEC 009 reporting form and instructions can be found on the FFIEC website at http://www.ffiec.gov/forms009_009a htm

**B.    "Immediate-Counterparty" and "Ultimate-Risk" Claims**

Claims are to be reported on an "immediate-counterparty" basis in Columns 1 through 8 and on an "ultimate-risk" basis in Columns 15 through 21. The obligor on an immediate-counterparty basis is the entity that issued the security or otherwise incurred the liability. The obligor of a claim on an ultimate-risk basis is any person, business, institution, or instrument that provides any of the types of credit protection described in Section II.D, "Required Risk Transfers" and Section II.G "Reporting Credit Derivatives." (Note, in particular, the rules given in Section II.D.5 concerning collateral.)

If full credit protection is provided by more than one source, the ultimate-risk claim should be reported in the sector and row of the residence of the highest rated credit enhancer.

**C.    Sector Definitions**

The following sector definitions are used for all columns of this report that provide sectoral distinctions:

(1) <u>Banks (Columns 1, 4, 9, 12, 15 and 18 of Schedule 1 and Column 1 of Schedule 2)</u> – The definition of banks is identical to "Banks, U.S. and Foreign" in the Report of Condition. Banks include commercial banks, savings banks, discount houses, and other similar institutions. Banks also include banking institutions owned by foreign governments, unless such institutions function as central banks or banks of issue, in which case they are treated as "public" institutions.

(2) <u>Public (Columns 2, 5, 10, 13, 16 and 19 of Schedule 1 and Column 2 of Schedule 2)</u> – The definition of the Public sector is identical to "Foreign Governments and Official Institutions" in the Report of Condition. Public sector institutions include:

- central, state, provincial and local governments and their departments, and agencies

- treasuries, ministries of finance, central banks, stabilization funds, exchange authorities, and diplomatic establishments

- those government owned banks, including development banks, that perform as an important part of their activities, the functions of a treasury, central bank, exchange control office, or stabilization fund

- international or regional organizations or subordinate or affiliated agencies thereof, created by treaty or convention between sovereign states, including the International Monetary Fund, the International Bank for Reconstruction and Development (World Bank), the Bank for International Settlements, the Inter-American Development Bank, and the United Nations

Banking institutions owned by a government that do not function as the central bank and/or bank of issue are excluded from the public sector and are to be reported as

"Banks." Other corporations that are owned by a government are to be reported as "Other."

(3) <u>Other (Columns 3, 6, 11, 14, 17 and 20 of Schedule 1 and Column 3 of Schedule 2)</u> – All persons, businesses, and institutions other than "banks" and "public," as defined above.

## D. Required Risk Transfers

Claims are redistributed from an "immediate-counterparty" basis to an "ultimate-risk" basis in Columns 9 through 14. The reporter is required to make the following risk transfers:

(1) Guarantees

Guarantees are formal legally binding commitments by a third party to repay a debt if the direct obligor fails to do so. Guarantees include financial and performance standby letters of credit and acceptances (for the amount of the participation sold). Documents that do not establish legal obligations, such as "comfort" letters, letters of awareness, or letters of intent, are not guarantees for the purpose of this report. Similarly, guarantees that do not cover transfer risk should not be considered a guarantee for the purposes of this report. Guarantees provided by the reporters' head office or other consolidated units of the reporter should not be considered a guarantee for the purposes of this report.

Guarantees providing protection to the respondent should result in the reallocation of the claim to the sector and country row of the provider of the guarantee. (Note: If the reporter provides a guarantee on a foreign credit, the amount of the guarantee should be reported in Column 23.)

(2) Insurance Policies

Insurance policies that guarantee payment of a claim if the borrower defaults or if non-convertibility occurs should be reallocated to the non-bank sector of the country of residence of the entity providing the insurance. However, limited purpose policies, such as "political risk insurance" policies should not be used as a basis for reallocation. (Note: If a reporter issues an insurance policy guaranteeing the payment of a claim if a foreign borrower defaults, the amount of the protection sold should be reported in Column 23.)

(3) Head Offices

For the purposes of this report, claims on a branch (but not on a subsidiary) of a banking organization are considered to be guaranteed by the head office of the organization, even without a legally binding agreement. Therefore, claims on branches should be reallocated to the bank sector in the country of the parent institution.

(4) Credit Derivatives

See Section II.G.

(5) Collateralized Claims

Collateral is treated as a "guarantee" of a claim if the collateral is: (a) tangible, liquid, and readily-realizable and (b) is both held and realizable outside of the country of residence of the borrower. Collateral can include investment grade debt instruments and regularly traded shares of stocks. In cases involving collateral other than stocks and debt securities, the sector and country of the "guaranteeing" party is the sector and country of residence of the institution holding the collateral. If the collateral is stocks or debt securities, the sector and country of the "guaranteeing" party is the sector and country of residence of the party issuing the security. **However, in the case of resale agreements and other similar financing agreements, the claims should be allocated based on the counterparty, not the underlying collateral.**

If the collateral consists of a basket of convertible currencies or investment grade securities of different countries, the exposure may be reported on the "Other" line (for example, "other Latin America") that most closely represents the geographical composition of the basket.

(6) Risk Participations

Loans and acceptances, where the accepting bank has sold a risk participation, are considered to be guaranteed by the purchaser of the participation for the amount of the participation sold.

Assets such as real estate and accounts receivable are not liquid or tangible assets. (Although only liquid, tangible, and readily realizable assets may be the basis of a reported risk transfer, the Federal banking agencies will consider the protection afforded by other assets to the reporting bank's country exposure claims when appraising each bank's country exposures.) In addition, a reporting institution that holds a claim with a repayment structure that insulates repayment from any form of transfer and country risk event, but the claim does not fall under one of the risk transfer categories above should contact their respective supervisory agency to consider if such claim can be redistributed in Columns 9 through 11.

### E. Cross-Border and Foreign-Office Claims on Local Residents

<u>Cross-border claims</u> of each reporter cover:
- all claims of its U.S. offices (including IBFs, Edge and Agreement corporations, and offices in Puerto Rico and U.S. territories and possessions) with residents of foreign countries, regardless of the currency in which the claim is denominated; *and*,

- all claims of each of its offices in a foreign country with residents of other foreign countries (i.e., countries other than the country in which the foreign office is located), regardless of the currency in which the claim is denominated.

Since the reports are on a fully consolidated bank (bank holding company) basis, cross-border claims exclude any claims against those foreign branches or foreign subsidiaries that are part of the consolidated bank (bank holding company). However, claims on unconsolidated subsidiaries or associated companies of the reporter should be reported. Thus, a consolidated bank basis report should include claims on foreign subsidiaries of the banks' parent holding company since these subsidiaries should not be included in consolidated reports of the bank. (Note: Net amounts due to or due from own related offices in other countries are shown as a separate memorandum item in Column 4 of Schedule 1.a.)

Foreign-office claims on local residents are all claims of the institution's foreign offices on residents of the country in which the foreign office is located.

Notes:

(1) Claims of a foreign office on a resident of the United States should not be reported as a cross-border claim (because the row for the United States should not be completed, except for Columns 9 through 14) nor as a foreign office claim on local residents (because they are not a claim on a resident of country in which a foreign office is located).

(2) The definition of "cross-border claims" and "foreign-office claims on local residents" is the same on an "immediate-counterparty" basis and an "ultimate-risk" basis. However, some claims may be categorized differently, or be placed in different sectors or country rows, because the sector or country of residence of the immediate obligor may differ from that of the ultimate obligor.

## F. "Local" vs. "Non-Local" Currency

A currency is considered to be a "local" currency of a country only if the country, directly or through a currency union, has the authority to issue that currency. Thus, U.S. dollars would not be considered to be the local currency of any country other than the United States. Euros would be considered to be the local currency of any country that is a member of the European Monetary Union, but of no other country.

## G. Reporting Credit Derivatives

Reporters should treat credit derivative contracts, (including credit default swaps and options, total return swaps and sovereign risk options), as guarantees for purposes of this report, if the institution considers the arrangement to be an effective risk transfer based on its internal criteria and the contract contains provisions to pass the transfer risk to the counterparty. A reporter's internal criteria should, at a minimum, include provisions that ensure the terms of credit derivatives provide an effective guarantee, even in the case of a maturity mismatch, prohibit clauses that reduce the effectiveness of the guarantee in the case of default, contain effectual events of default, and reference the same legal entity as the obligor.

Claims for which credit derivatives form an effective risk transfer should be reallocated to the sector and country of residence of the entity that is providing the protection.

Credit derivatives are reported in three places in this report:

(1) On Schedule 1, <u>the notional value of credit protection purchased</u> by the respondent can result in both inward and outward risk transfers, as the credit risk is shifted from the sector and/or country row of the immediate counterparty to the sector and/or country row of the credit protection seller.

(2) On Schedule 1, <u>the notional value of credit protection sold</u> by the respondent is reported in Column 23 (only). In each country row of Column 23, the reporter should report the notional value of the credit protection sold against the risk of default or other credit event by the ultimate obligor of the referenced credit.

(3) On Schedule 2, claims arising from the fair value of credit derivative contracts (including the fair value of protection purchased and protection sold) are reported against the country of the counterparty, along with claims arising from the fair value of other derivative contracts.

**Appendix B**

*[Editor's Note: The following is an abridged version of the preamble to the original* **Federal Register** *publication of the final ATRR regulation. The current version of the regulation can be found at 12 CFR Parts 28, 211 and 347]*

DEPARTMENT OF THE TREASURY
Comptroller of the Currency

FEDERAL RESERVE SYSTEM

FEDERAL DEPOSIT INSURANCE CORPORATION

12 CFR Parts 20, 211 and 351
Allocated Transfer Risk Reserve

49 FR 5587

February 13, 1984

**ACTION:** Joint notice of final rules and request for additional comments.

**SUMMARY:** These regulations require banking institutions to establish special reserves against the risks presented in certain international assets when the Federal banking agencies (Board of Governors of the Federal Reserve System ("Board"), Comptroller of the Currency and Federal Deposit Insurance Corporation) determine that such reserves are necessary. In particular, they are intended to require banking institutions to recognize uniformly the transfer risk and diminished value of international assets which have not been serviced over a protracted period of time. These regulations implement one aspect of the joint program of the Federal banking agencies to strengthen the supervisory and regulatory framework relating to foreign lending by U.S. banking institutions, incorporated in section 905(a) of the International Lending Supervision Act of 1983.

It is important that this provision of law be implemented expeditiously for banking regulatory and supervisory purposes. Accordingly, the regulations will be effective upon publication.

Further regulations implementing other provisions of the International Lending Supervision Act of 1983 will be issued separately.

**EFFECTIVE DATE:** February 13, 1984.

Following are the major topics raised in the comments and the agencies' responses thereto:

## (1) Assets to be covered by the Allocated Transfer Risk Reserve (ATRR)

The proposed regulations required banking institutions to establish an ATRR for "specified international assets," and defined "international assets" to mean those assets included in Country Exposure Report forms (FFIEC No. 009). Numerous commenters suggested clarification of the definition of international assets or exemption for certain categories of assets or for specific assets.

The agencies intend that an ATRR will be required only for international assets subject to transfer risk. International assets subject to transfer risk associated with the country of residence of the obligor normally do not include, for example, (1) assets guaranteed by a resident of a foreign country different from that of the direct obligor; (2) certain collateralized assets; (3) commitments; and (4) assets of a foreign office of the banking institution payable in local currency for which the foreign office has equivalent local currency liabilities. (The foregoing examples are described in more detail in the Instructions to Country Exposure Report forms.)

The banking agencies also will consider whether the performance characteristics of certain categories of assets are such that no ATRR is warranted against those assets (e.g., assets on which debt service has been maintained with little or no interruption.)

In this connection, in line with the suggestions of several commenters on the treatment of new loans, an ATRR normally would not be required initially for net new lending when the additional loans are made in countries implementing economic adjustment programs, such as programs approved by the International Monetary Fund, designed to correct the countries' economic difficulties in an orderly manner. Such new lending under appropriate circumstances may strengthen the functioning of the adjustment process, help to improve the quality of outstanding credit, and thus be consistent with the objectives of the program of improved supervision of international lending. Whether an ATRR subsequently is required for those new loans would be determined by the agencies on the basis of performance and continued inapplicability generally of the criteria for establishment of an ATRR.

## (2) Applicability to nonbank and foreign subsidiaries

The proposed regulations would apply to a banking institution and its subsidiaries, and "subsidiary" was defined to mean an organization of which a banking institution has control or holds 25 percent or more of the voting shares. Two issues raised by the comments were (1) whether the provision should apply to minority-owned nonbank subsidiaries; and (2) whether it should apply to foreign bank subsidiaries of banking institutions.

On the issue of whether minority-owned subsidiaries should be covered, several of the commenters reasoned that a banking institution with a 25 percent interest in an entity may not be able to compel that entity to comply with the regulation and should not be held responsible for the entity's accounting methods. Several commenters proposed that the regulations cover only those nonbank subsidiaries that are consolidated with the parent banking institution under Generally Accepted Accounting Principles (GAAP). Objections also were raised to applying the regulations to foreign subsidiaries.

In light of these comments, the agencies determined that each "banking institution" is subject to the regulations on a consolidated basis. "Banking institution" is defined in the regulations as a domestic bank, Edge or Agreement corporation engaged in banking, and bank holding company. Other than the foregoing banking institutions, subsidiaries need not separately comply with these regulations. The effect of this rule for foreign bank subsidiaries is that specific reserves against, or write-downs of, international assets, taken from current earnings of the foreign bank, will be incorporated in the parent banking institution's consolidated financial statement.

For banks, consolidation should be in accordance with the procedures and tests of significance set forth in the instructions for preparation of Consolidated Reports of Condition and Income (currently, FFIEC Nos. 031, 032, 033, 034). For bank holding companies, the consolidation shall be in accordance with the principles set forth in the "Instructions to the Bank Holding Company Financial Supplement to Report F.R. Y-6" (Form F.R. Y-9). Edge and Agreement Corporations should file in accordance with the "Instructions for the Preparation of Report of Condition for Edge and Agreement Corporations" (Form F.R. 2886b).

In applying the foregoing rules to bank holding companies under section 910(a)(2) of the act, the Board has deemed such action appropriate to promote uniform application of section 905(a) of the Act and to prevent evasions thereof.

### (3) Criteria for Requiring an ATRR

In determining whether an ATRR is warranted for particular international assets, the agencies are directed by statute to apply the following factors: (1) Whether the quality of a banking institution's assets has been impaired by a protracted inability of public or private obligors to pay or (2) whether no definite prospects exist for the orderly restoration of debt service. Some commenters urged more specific criteria; others were concerned that the criteria were not flexible enough. Most of the commenters, however, generally agreed that the statutory criteria are reasonable. The agencies consider the statutory criteria to be appropriate because they provide guidance as to when an ATRR is required, while allowing the agencies to take into account a sufficient range of factors in making their determinations.

### (4) Percentage Norms

Under the proposed regulations, the initial year's provision for the ATRR would be ten percent of the principal amount of the specified international assets, or a greater or lesser percentage as determined by the banking agencies. In subsequent years, the agencies would review the assets concerned and determine whether additional reserves are required. The proposal provided for a reserve based on such review in the subsequent periods of 15 percent, or a higher or lower percentage as determined necessary by the banking agencies. In the preamble to the proposed regulation, the agencies specifically asked for comment on these percentages.

Some commenters thought the percentages were too low, and some considered them too high. Several were opposed to the establishment of any percentage norms, primarily on the ground that the appropriate percentages should be determined by the agencies in each case and that agency flexibility in making this determination should be preserved. However, a substantial number of comments supported the proposed percentages as reasonable.

The agencies believe that the norms contained in the regulations provide reasonable guidance to banking institutions of the likely ATRR requirements, yet the regulations give the agencies discretion to modify these percentages on a case-by-case basis as factors warrant.

### (5) Treatment of ATRR Accounting

The provision in the proposed regulations eliciting most comment was the section allowing banking institutions to write down an asset in the same amount as required for the ATRR, instead of setting up the ATRR, but requiring the banking institution, in that case, to replenish the Allowance for Possible Loan Losses (APLL) out of current earnings by the amount written down. Commenters suggested that if a banking institution chooses to write down an asset instead of establishing an ATRR, the APLL should be replenished only to the extent necessary to restore it to a level adequate to reflect the remaining risks in the loan portfolio.

The commenters pointed out several problems they see with the replenishment provision as it was proposed: it could put banks that already have charged earnings at a disadvantage vis-à-vis those banks that have made no comparable provisions; it could thus discourage conservative practices; and, as a result of inconsistency with GAAP, it could distort financial statements and cause them to be qualified by accountants.

In light of these comments, the agencies have determined that, consistent with prudent banking practices and GAAP, replenishment of the APLL will be required to the extent necessary to restore it to a level which adequately provides for the estimated losses inherent in the loan portfolio. The agencies wish to emphasize, however, that it remains the responsibility of bank management and external auditors to recognize, and management to provide adequately for, any significant deterioration in the value of assets and this responsibility is in no way lessened as a result of the agencies' adoption of this recommendation.

Several commenters also sought further clarification of the alternative accounting treatment under which an ATRR would not be required if comparable amounts of the assets had been written down. Some comments stated that the regulations should clarify the treatment of interest payments which have been applied to the loan balance. They suggested that the regulations specify that such reductions of principal should be considered write-downs for purposes of the regulations. Another issue was the treatment of write-downs of assets in prior reporting periods. The final regulations clarify that write-downs in prior periods, as well as reductions in principal as described above, which are tantamount to write-downs, are acceptable alternatives to establishment of an ATRR.

Another issue raised in connection with the alternative accounting treatment was whether a write-down of an asset for commercial risk will be treated the same as a write-down for transfer risk reasons. The final regulations have been clarified to state that an ATRR applies to the principal amount of each specified international asset in the percentage required. Accordingly, a write-down of any such asset for commercial risk can be included in the amount of a write-down which satisfies a required ATRR for that particular asset but not for specified assets in the aggregate.

One commenter suggested that the regulations be clarified to indicate that a banking institution may transfer to the ATRR any amount specifically allocated in the APLL for the assets subject to the ATRR. The agencies consider this approach an acceptable method of implementing the ATRR requirement, particularly since a banking institution could in any event write down an asset by a charge to its APLL rather than a charge to current earnings in the period the write-down is taken. However, in either instance, the APLL must be replenished to the extent necessary to restore it to a level that adequately provides for the estimated losses inherent in the loan portfolio.

Finally, clarification was sought, and the agencies have so provided in the final regulations, that a banking institution may reduce an established ATRR not only if the banking agencies determine it may be reduced, but also where the institution decides to write down the assets involved.

### (6) Timing of ATRR implementation

Several commenters requested that notifications of ATRR requirements be made on a timely basis relative to banking institutions' reporting and filing dates for their financial statements. The banking agencies intend to make every effort, in providing notice of ATRR requirements, to accommodate these concerns, recognizing the importance, however, of prompt implementation of section 905(a) of the Act and initial establishment of the ATRR.

### (7) Consultation with banking institutions

Several commenters stressed the importance of regular consultation with the affected banking institutions by the agencies before establishing the ATRR. One commenter suggested that concerns about a particular country should be discussed in the course of the normal bank examination process to evaluate all factors concerning the obligors' ability to pay. Discussions of foreign country exposure and transfer risk are a part of the ongoing examination process and efforts will be made by the agencies to strengthen consultations in this context.

### (8) Applicability of the Act to U.S. branches and agencies of foreign banks

Comment was requested on whether and the extent to which foreign banks should be subject to this and other provisions of the Act. The period for comment on these general issues remains open to permit foreign banks adequate time to respond, and the final regulations do not apply to U.S. branches, agencies or commercial lending company subsidiaries of foreign banking organizations.

### (9) Other comments

Questions were raised concerning the confidentiality of the agencies' determinations of the international assets specified as subject to the ATRR and the applicable reserve percentages. As is customary, such notifications are conveyed as confidential examination information to each affected U.S. banking institution by its primary federal banking supervisor.

Several commenters stated that the regulation should not govern disclosures under the federal securities laws. In this connection, the federal banking agencies understand that the staff of the Securities and Exchange Commission will provide guidance to registrants concerning appropriate disclosure of ATRR requirements in filings with the SEC.

**Appendix C**

## OFFICE OF THE COMPTROLLER OF THE CURRENCY
## BOARD OF GOVERNORS OF THE FEDERAL RESERVE SYSTEM
## FEDERAL DEPOSIT INSURANCE CORPORATION

### October 30, 1992

**TO THE CHIEF EXECUTIVE OFFICERS OF BANKS WITH INTERNATIONAL ASSETS**

A question has arisen as to the appropriate Call Report treatment for debt-for-equity or debt-for-debt exchanges by banks that involve countries for which the Interagency Country Exposure Review Committee (ICERC) evaluation of transfer risk has led to the establishment of an Allocated Transfer Risk Reserve (ATRR) requirement. In such exchanges, banks swap developing country debt for equity securities or debt securities under government-sponsored programs. Specifically, does the ATRR requirement only apply to banks' existing loan exposures or does it also apply to those exposures that take the form of equity or debt securities obtained through such conversions?

In order to assure uniformity, the Office of the Comptroller of the Currency, the Federal Reserve and Federal Deposit Insurance Corporation are clarifying their policy. It is the position of the agencies that:

- Transfer risk may continue to exist for an exposure converted to (exchanged for) assets in the form of equity or debt securities. Under both generally accepted accounting principles (GAAP) and regulatory reporting requirements, a debt exchange must be reported at fair value. However, the initial recorded value of a security received in a debt conversion cannot exceed the carrying value of the converted loan exposure, net of any applicable ATRR.

- Securities that are held in a bank's trading account (i.e., that have an active and liquid market) and are actively traded by the bank in a dollar or other hard currency market would be (as at present) exempt from ATRR application. Such securities would be carried at market value. In all other cases, including both securities held for investment purposes and those held for eventual sale in a longer time frame (e.g., certain Debts Previously Contracted (DPC) and Regulation K holdings), the ATRR framework would apply UNLESS the ICERC determines in its review of transfer risk for a particular country that grounds exist for a more favorable treatment of securities obtained in officially sanctioned debt conversion programs in that country.

- Specifically, the ICERC would consider relevant information on officially-sponsored debt conversion programs in a given country in order to reach a judgment as to whether transfer risk for the resulting securities may be sufficiently lower than for the country's external financial obligations as a whole and whether this warrants a full or partial exemption from the ATRR requirements.

- In reaching its conclusions, the ICERC would consider, among other things,

  - the existence of a clearly different income and capital repatriation program for securities obtained through debt conversions relative to repatriation policies existing for sovereign debt service.
  - performance of the country under such programs to date, or more generally for debt or equity securities vs. loan obligations, in permitting the repatriation of income and capital.
  - other relevant evidence that transfer risk for the securities obtained under the exchange program is in fact lower than that for the country's external financial obligations as a whole.

- When the ICERC has determined that debt conversion programs of a particular country can provide reduced transfer risk, examiners will verify that transactions conducted by individual banks qualify for exemption from the ATRR within the ICERC-established framework.

- In addition to assessing transfer risk, examiners will also review each security holding to assure that the carrying value is recorded in accordance with GAAP and regulatory reporting requirements as well as normal examination procedures applied to bank investments in securities. In particular, in cases involving securities acquired through asset swaps rather than for cash, examiners will determine that the initial valuation is supported by evidence of fair value. In doing so, examiners will consider, among other things,

  - similar transactions for cash.
  - estimated cash flows from the security received. Any projections used to justify an initial valuation higher than the secondary market price of the debt exchanged must be supportable based on historic performance or other empirical grounds.
  - the initial valuation of the investment by other purchasers, participants, or shareholders.
  - the market value of similar debt or equity investments.

- currency restrictions, if any, affecting dividends, the sale of the investment, or the repatriation of capital.

- With respect to equity investments that are carried by the bank using the equity method of accounting, the ATRR is deemed to apply to the entire investment including any increases in carrying value reflecting equity income, unless ICERC determines that grounds exist for more favorable treatment of the equity securities and related equity income, as detailed above.

- As with other assets, examiners will determine whether such investments should be classified or criticized for reasons of commercial risk and assigned the more severe of the commercial or country risk classifications in evaluating a bank's asset quality.

www.ingramcontent.com/pod-product-compliance
Lightning Source LLC
Chambersburg PA
CBHW081809170526
45167CB00008B/3384